THE WORLD'S LAST STEAM
CHINA

CHRIS DAVIES

Published by Key Books
An imprint of Key Publishing Ltd
PO Box 100
Stamford
Lincs PE19 1XQ

www.keypublishing.com

ISBN 978 1 913295 97 4

20 21 22 23 24   10 9 8 7 6 5 4 3 2 1

Typeset by SJmagic DESIGN SERVICES, India.

Title Page Image: The winter sun dips below the horizon at the Wulong dump as an SY Class locomotive, laden with mine waste, slowly makes its way up the incline to dispose of the waste. 3 December 2015.

Contents Page Image: JS 8225 arrives at the wash plant with another load of coal for processing – the Tian Shan Mountains are in the distance. 6 December 2015.

CONTENTS

AUTHOR'S NOTE

I am old enough to just about remember the existence of steam trains in Britain. My earliest recollection is of a steam engine heading a freight train at Newport station. I lived in Newport briefly as a child and remember my brothers, my mum and I were about to board a train at Newport station when I was mesmerised by the sight of a magnificent steam locomotive. I also have vivid memories of steam locomotives working at Cadoxton in Barry. I recall, during the long summer evenings, spending the night at my grandparents' house in Barry and seeing steam engines carrying out shunting duties at the docks from my bedroom window, when I should have been asleep in bed! Soon after, steam was phased out in South Wales.

After graduating from university in 1979, I started my first job as a geologist in Africa in1980. I was based in Kabwe in Zambia, which in those days was the principal railway centre in Zambia. To my amazement, at the railway yard near my office, two Zambia Railways steam locomotives could be seen shunting regularly. I desperately wanted to photograph them, but security was tight in those days, and I ran this risk of being arrested, so I resisted the temptation.

Later, while still based in Zambia, I went to a conference in Kimberly in South Africa. I recall seeing numerous steam locomotives on freight trains not far from the hotel where I was staying. It did not occur to me to try and get some shots though, something I very much regret, as I was tied up with the conference and time was short.

I am not sure why I am fascinated by steam trains, but I guess it is a combination of things. They rekindle fond memories as a child, a time when I was far too young to even contemplate photographing them. The sound, the smell of burning coal, the billowing steam and smoke, all combine to give the impression of a living creature rather than a man-made machine, so different from diesel locomotives, which are inanimate by comparison. I certainly do not profess to be an expert on steam locomotives, far from it, but I do love photographing them.

I am in absolute awe of the people, in the UK and other countries around the world, who run and maintain our heritage railways so that we can enjoy getting a real feel of how the railways were during the steam era. However, nothing beats a real working steam locomotive as what you see is what you get.

I have known about the existence of steam trains in China for some time, but it never occurred to me to visit the country to see them. I did not know where to go or how to get around, and I lacked the confidence to do it on my own without others to help me. However, this was all to change in August 2015, when an advert in the *Railway Magazine* (a monthly British railway magazine aimed at the railway enthusiast) by Germany-based FarRail Tours caught my eye. Captioned, 'Last Winter Steam in China – the Scraping the Barrel Tour', I read it with keen interest. After some deliberation, I decided if I wanted to see real working steam locomotives in action, perhaps for the last time ever, this could be my only chance.

I got in touch with Bernd Seiler of FarRail Tours and signed up for his tour from 29 November to 13 December 2015. On offer were the last places in China where one was guaranteed to see steam engines still in action: Sandaoling, in north-west China, a large open-pit coal mine worked by JS Class locomotives; Baiyin, situated approximately 1,000km south-west of Beijing, which had one of the last steam-hauled passenger trains in the world; and Fuxin, a coal-mining city approximately 500km north-east of Beijing, which had SY Class locomotives in action. It was an utterly amazing experience and a lot of the images in this book are from that first visit.

However, the steam trains continued to operate in China after 2015 and so did Bernd Seiler's FarRail tours. In late 2016, I learned that, having just returned from a trip to Sandaoling in December of that year, he was offering yet another one in February 2017 (before the steam trains might disappear altogether) but with a difference. This time, he was also proposing the chance to visit another Chinese location with working steam trains, Wu Jiu, in Inner Mongolia. It was a punt to trek all the way to Inner Mongolia as there was no guarantee that we would see the trains in action in these remote parts, but the allure of going to another location in China, as well as revisiting Sandaoling, was the catalyst for signing up for another trip on 11 to 22 February 2017.

The images featured in the book are from the visits I made with FarRail in 2015 and 2017. They were taken using a Fujifilm compact SLR camera, the X-E1 and XT-10 models. All the images were shot as RAW files and processed using Photoshop. A few are rendered in black and white, which can be a powerful medium for portraying a mood or feeling.

I have enjoyed putting this book together and every effort has been made to keep it as accurate as possible but no doubt there may be some mistakes, for which I apologise. The research has been based on my own field notes, from information gleaned from the web and from the few published books on Chinese steam. I would be more than happy to hear from anyone with any comments.

Acknowledgements

I should like to thank Bernd Seiler of FarRail tours for organising the trips to China, without whom, none of the images featured would have been possible. His unbounding enthusiasm and knowledge of the railways is the reason this book has been possible.

The information used to compile the book has come from several sources. The internet has some excellent sites, two in particular: Duncan Cotterill's Railography website on Chinese steam (http://www.railography. co.uk/news/files/category-china---steam.php), which is packed full of information with trip reports, locomotive lists, locomotive profiles (history) and news, and is illustrated with some wonderful images; and SY Country (http://www.internationalsteam.co.uk/syc/qjc/content.htm), which was established by Dave Fielding in October 2006 and transferred to Rob Dickinson's International Steam website on 17 October 2018, and is also extremely informative and was a great help. FarRail tours website (http://www.farrail.com) has also been invaluable with its trip reports, blog site and amazing images.

I also consulted several books featuring Chinese steam, which have been especially useful. John Tickner, Gordon Edgar and Adrian Freeman's photographic journal titled, *China – The World's Last Steam Railway* (Artist's and Photographers' Press Ltd, 2008), with its superb photographs and informative text, not to mention some of the amazing tales the authors relate about getting the pictures in the first place in remote parts of China, has been an inspiration for this book. Keith Strickland's book, *The Best of Steam – Railway of the World in Photographs* (History Press Limited, 2015), has also provided an invaluable contribution, together with Colin Garratt's book, *100 Years of Steam – Classic Steam* (Colour Library Direct, 1997). Finally, *The Encyclopaedia of Trains and Locomotives* (Thunder Bay Press, 2003), has been a useful reference guide for Chinese steam locomotives. I should also like to thank Mr Yifan Jiang, who was kind enough to provide some useful information on Wu Jiu.

Finally, I should like to thank Key Publishing, who approached me to compile the book last November, and my wife, Claire, who was kind enough to read through the manuscript and make amendments where necessary.

Chris Davies
23 June 2020

Night-time photography was particularly rewarding at the depot in Fuxin where locomotives would take on water and sand in preparation for the new shift. In this scene, SY 1397 is taking on water whilst the ash is raked out. 1 December 2015.

INTRODUCTION

Snapshot

China was the last country in the world to build and operate steam locomotives. The expansion of the railways after the Second World War resulted in motive power shortages, so many older engines continued longer in service than they might otherwise have done. By the early 1980s, there were an estimated 10,000 operational steam locomotives in China. Even so, the country did not have an outright steam policy. During the 1980s and 1990s, diesel and electric locomotives started to replace the steam engines on the main lines. This led to the number in service being substantially reduced as the millennium approached, but there were still an estimated 4,000 in service on China Rail by the mid-1990s. The last of the locomotives were finally withdrawn from China Rail in 2003. Since that time, some continued to operate heavy freight trains on local railways for a short while, but most were deployed for use on the country's industrial railways. This trend continued into the first decade of the 21st century, but after that, numbers declined substantially and were confined to just a handful of industrial locations.

From the 1980s, China has been a magnet for steam enthusiasts from all over the world but there is now only one location that exists where one is guaranteed to see steam engines in action. This is Sandaoling in north-west China, which has been fittingly described as the 'last steam show on earth'. However, its days of steam operation are numbered.

A Brief History of Chinese Steam

After the First World War, the Americans supplied main-line 2-8-2 Mikados, one of America's most popular engines, to the South Manchuria Railway in China. During the Japanese occupation, which started in the early 1930s, the Chinese railways played a vital part in the transportation of coal and iron ore, using the Mikados imported from the USA. The design was subsequently adapted to build JF locomotives, used for freight trains, which remained in use until 2006. The 2-6-2 PL2 Class, an industrial locomotive used by China Rail, was originally built in 1935 by the Japanese (Nippon Sharyō) for the South Manchuria Railway and was designated the Pureni Class. The YJ designs were related to the pre-war Japanese PL2 Class and built from 1958 to 1961. The SL6, a heavy Pacific design from the 1930s that was originally built by the Japanese, was the most numerous class of steam passenger locomotive in China, with 422 eventually being built. The lighter Pacific design, the SL3, also originally built by the Japanese, was likewise used for passenger services.

Following the Second World War, the railways were in poor shape, but the large fleet of dependable Japanese locomotives continued to be produced. China also received locomotives as reconstruction aid, including the United States Army Transportation Corps S160 Class 2-8-0 steam locomotives, which were designed for heavy freight work in Europe during the Second World War, and the Anshan XK2 0-6-0 engines, which were also used to support the war effort in Europe. Russia also helped with the introduction of FD 2-10-2 locomotives, built by the Soviet Union between 1931 and 1942 and sold to China in the late 1950s and early 1960s. The RM Pacific, dating back to the late 1950s, was a 4-6-2 main-line general-purpose engine. About 250 of the class were constructed and were still in service in the early 1980s.

In the last years of steam in China, three classes of steam locomotives were mostly in use: the QJ Class 2-10-2s, the smaller JS Class 2-8-2s and the slightly smaller SY Class 2-8-2s. Although the designs represented the ultimate in Chinese innovation and steam development, they were essentially reminiscent of the type of locomotive used on the American railroads some 90 years earlier.

The QJ Class 2-10-2 locomotives were China's most important American derivative. They were built by the Dalian and Tangshan workshops and were a common sight on the main line until steam was phased out in 2003. Over 3,000 were believed to be in service and they were the principal main-line freight trains that replaced the JF and FD classes. They are thought to be based on the Russian LV design. The early production and prototypes of the class were designated HP and became known as the QJ Class in 1971. The QJs were gradually replaced by diesel locomotives from the late 1980s through to the 1990s.

The JS Class Mikado was a development of the JF Class and remained in production from the late 1950s until the end of main-line steam production in 1988. The SY Class locomotives were mainly used for industrial purposes and were the last locomotives to be built in China, with production ending in 1999. During the last years of steam operation on the main line, the number of locomotives in service dropped substantially and steam traction officially ended on China Rail in 2003. As mentioned earlier, some engines remained in use for a little longer on the local railways, but many of China Rail's ex-steam locomotives ended up at industrial complexes, such as coal mines and steelworks. These were mainly JS and SY classes, sold during the 1990s. A few QJs also survived for industrial use until 2010.

I take my hat off to those steam enthusiasts who had the drive and motivation to visit China during the steam era, braving the extreme winter temperatures and travelling to remote locations where few, if any, foreigners visited. There are some amazing photographs and stories from this time in the pre-digital era, notably, John Tickner, Gordon Edgar and Adrian Freeman's superb photographic journal, *China – The World's Last Steam Railway*, published in 2008.

Perhaps one of the most popular places to visit in recent years was the Ji-Tong Railway in Inner Mongolia. Although steam officially ended on the China Rail main line in 2003, the 945km-long line continued to operate heavy freight trains using QJ locomotives. A total of 100 QJs were purchased from China Rail by the Ji-Tong Railway, in preference to acquiring a new fleet of diesel locomotives, to save costs. The line opened as recently as 1995 and remained in use, entirely under steam, until 2005. A favourite route for photographers was from Daban to Haoluhu, which included the Jingpeng Pass, a stunning scenic part of the line where double-headed QJs worked long freight trains along horseshoe curves, tunnels and viaducts.

Industrial Steam

After the end of steam on China Rail, steam continued at industrial sites around the country, mainly mining operations and steel works, using the ex-China Rail steam locomotives. The majority were deployed at China's numerous coal mines (both open pit and underground). It is worth noting that China is the largest producer and consumer of coal in the world and has substantial deposits, particularly in Inner Mongolia, the largest coal-producing province. In 2018, China produced some 3.5 billion tonnes of coal and it is the largest user of electricity generated from coal-fired power stations.

In 2007, it was estimated that around 400 steam locomotives were still active on the industrial railways, with the greatest concentration deployed at two large open-pit coal operations: Jalainur in north China and Sandaoling in north-west China.

Jalainur, located near Manzhouli in Inner Mongolia, close to the border with Russia, was a substantial opencast operation with up to 30 SY Class locomotives working on a 24/7 basis. The vast rich coal seams were easy to exploit by open pit, due to low stripping ratios, allowing ease of mining. A favourite activity amongst enthusiasts was to look down into the deep hole to see the exhausts of numerous locomotives working the benches way down in the pit. The operation closed in 2009.

The other, at Sandaoling, located in north-west China, is still operational to this day and is the last steam-worked opencast coal mine in the world. Until recent years, it too had 20 or more steam locomotives (mainly JS but some SY Class) working, which have now been reduced to a few operational JS Class locomotives (ten or fewer) as the mine comes to the end of its productive life.

Whilst a handful of other operations continued to use steam in recent years, they are no longer active. China's drive to reduce pollution and combat climate change from burning coal has resulted in some of the operations replacing their steam fleet in favour of the cleaner and easier to maintain diesels, or making use of road transport instead. In addition, the financial viability of keeping some of the loss-making deep underground coal mines operational and the Chinese government's recent strict policy on mine safety have both played their part in determining the fate of some operations and, with them, their industrial steam railways.

In recent years, the Chinese government has tightened the regulations on mining safety in an effort to reduce the appalling death toll from coal mine accidents. Consequently, many small-scale coal mines that have been deemed unsafe have closed in recent years, together with their steam-operated industrial railways. This was the case at Pingzhuang in Inner Mongolia, where a mining accident led to the tragic loss of 30 miners in 2016. The operation was suspended together with its industrial railway, which was still utilising SY Class locomotives.

In August 2016, the Wulong Colliery at Fuxin in Liaoning Province was declared bankrupt. The operation shut down virtually overnight and with it, its steam railway, which was still operating several SY Class locomotives.

Steam rail operations in China are now facing extinction. Sandaoling is the only industrial operation remaining in China where steam locomotives still operate 24 hours a day. Other than this, a few pockets of steam locomotives may still survive elsewhere for shunting purposes, but with the lack of activity and limited photographic opportunities, visits to such locations would likely not be worthwhile. For example, the Wu Jiu coal mining area in Inner Mongolia, which I visited in 2017 and is featured in the book, still had one active SY Class locomotive serving several deep coal mines (collieries) in late 2017. However, the locomotive only operates on an intermittent basis, so there is no guarantee of seeing it in action. The current status of the operation is unknown.

The table on page 10 lists the operations where steam trains have been active over the past decade or so. The list has been compiled from information gleaned from Flickr, blog sites and the web but is by no means exhaustive. Rather, it is intended as a guide to illustrate some of the industrial locations that have used steam traction in recent years.

Surviving Operations Under Steam 2009–20

Name	Location	Activity	Status	Traction
Sandaoling	Xinjiang Province, north-west china	Coal mining (open pit/deep mines), currently active	Active	JS
Wu Jiu	Inner Mongolia, north-east China	Coal mining (deep mines), infrequent activity	Unknown – active in late 2017	SY
Baiyin	Gansu Province, north-central China	Copper, lead and zinc mines/smelters	Steam ended in early 2017	SY
Fuxin	Liaoning Province, north-east China	Coal mining (deep mines)	Steam ended in 2016	SY
Pingzhuang	Inner Mongolia, north-east China	Coal mining	Steam ended in 2016	
Guangshan	Liaoning Province, north-east China	Coal mining	Steam ended in 2010	SY
Jalainur	Inner Mongolia, north-east China	Coal mining (open pit/deep mines)	Steam ended in 2009	SY
Diaobingshan Tiefa Coal Railway	Liaoning Province, north-east China	Coal mining	Steam ended in 2014	
Beitai	Liaoning Province, north-east China	Steel works	Steam ended in 2012	SY
Jixi Coal Railway	Heilongjiang Province, north-east China.	Coal mining	Steam ended in 2010	SY

The Work Horses

Two classes of steam locomotives were operational on my visits to China: the JS and SY classes.

The JS class (*Jiàn Shè* – 'Construction' or 'Development') is still in operation at Sandaoling. A 2-8-2 tender steam locomotive, it was manufactured for use on main-line freight and passenger lines as well as for shunting. The locomotives were built in cooperation with the USSR and went into production at Dalian in 1957. A modified design, the JS 'B's, produced in Datong from the mid-1980s, were easier to maintain and suitable for shunting services. The last were built in 1988, and they saw service throughout the whole of China until the end of steam on China Rail.

JS/SY Class Attributes

Class Designation	JS (建设)	SY (上游)
Descriptive Name	*Jian She* ('Construction')	*Shang You* ('Aiming High')
Number Series	JS 5001–6135 JS 6201–6558 JS 80018423	SY 00011772 SY 20012024 SY 30013024
Builder	Dalian, Qishuyan, Datong – 1957 to 1965 and 1981 to 1988	Tangshan, Sifang, Tongling, Jinan, Changchun
Number built	1,916	1,820
Wheel Configuration	2-8-2	2-8-2
Boiler Pressure	15 bar/220psi	13.7 bar/200psi
Length	23.2 metres	21.6 metres
Overall Weight	173t	142t
Maximum speed	85km/hour	80km/hour

The locomotives in use at Sandaoling date from the 1980s Datong production line. They would originally have had smoke deflectors which have since been removed.

JS Class 2-8-2 Locomotive at work at Sandaoling, Xinjiang Province.

The SY Class locomotive (*Shàng Yóu* – 'Aiming High') was China's standard industrial locomotive. Over 1,800 of these useful light 2-8-2s were built between 1960 and 1999, the vast majority at Tangshan. They were the last of the Chinese steam classes to enter production and the SY was the last steam locomotive to be built in the world. The design appears to be based on the earlier Japanese-built JF6 Class 2-8-2, which itself was based on a locomotive type built by the American Locomotive Company in the 1920s for use in Japanese-occupied Manchuria in 1934. Hence, it has an American look to it.

The SY Class was extensively used on China's industrial lines and was rarely used on the main lines. Several hundred remained in service into the 21st century, principally in the coal and steel industries. It was also one of the last steam locomotives in the world to haul commuter trains on the industrial lines, ferrying workers to the mine and industrial sites. They were seen at Baiyin, Fuxin and Wu Jiu.

Below: **SY Class 2-8-2 Locomotive at work at Wu Jiu, Inner Mongolia.**

Locations Visited.

CHAPTER 1
SANDAOLING STEAM SWANSONG

Sandaoling, situated 60km west of Hami in north-west China in Xinjiang Province (officially designated the Uygur Autonomous Region) on the fringes of the Gobi Desert, is the last place in the world where steam trains operate 24 hours a day, seven days a week.

Opened in 1962, Sandaoling is the largest open-pit coal mine in north-west China and is some 6km long by up to 0.9 km wide. Its annual production reached three million tonnes at its peak when more than 30 locomotives were running each day, hauling coal out of the opencast mine and across the desert to the nearby collieries. There are two collieries (underground mines), Yijing and Erjing, near the pit. While Yijing is no longer operational, Erjing still is and is served by rail, using steam locomotives, which is a separate operation from the open pit. A third deep mine, Shadunzi, located approximately 12km west of the open pit, is also served by the industrial rail network, using diesel locomotives. The Sandaoling rail network is linked to China Rail exchange sidings at Liushuquan, approximately 13km south-east of Nanzhan.

As recently as 2010, both JS and SY Class locomotives were in use at Sandaoling and up to 25 locomotives were in service. A large part of the operation involved removing mine waste using locomotives stabled at the yard at Xibolizhan, where it was dumped using a series of spoil disposal lines in an area south-west of the open pit. However, the trains ceased operating in 2014 when trucks were used to remove the spoil instead. Since then, the number of locomotives in service has decreased significantly. During my visits in 2015 and 2017, around ten JS steam

locomotives were in operation but the SY Class locomotives were no longer in use.

Of those ten JS Class locomotives in operation, four were deployed for use in the open pit and one was used to ferry workers to the pit during shift change, for shunting duties and as a spare locomotive. Three locomotives were used to service the colliery at Erjing and two were undergoing repairs at the workshop. Locomotives in service at the time of my visits were as follows:

Locomotive Number	Location
JS 8081	Sandaoling
JS 8190	Sandaoling
JS 8225	Sandaoling
JS 8167	Sandaoling
JS 8078	Sandaoling
JS 8197	Sandaoling
JS 8173	Sandaoling
JS 8366	Nanzhan
JS 8089	Nanzhan
JS 6204	Nanzhan
JS 8314	Nanzhan
JS 8358	Nanzhan
JS 8053	Nanzhan

Sandaoling is a push-pull operation. Empty tipper wagons are pushed back from the disposal points (where the coal is unloaded for processing) into the open pit and on to the loading pads at Xikeng. Loaded trains haul the coal, chimney first, back to the disposal points. About 15 tons of coal per shift is required to power the locomotives.

The JS Class locomotives have a crew of four men. The driver, an assistant driver, a fireman and a flagman. The driver sits on the left-hand side of the cab, the assistant usually stays on the right and the fireman shovels coal. The flagman, whose task is to signal the driver, leads a solitary existence in a caboose at the other end of the train. With a fishtail wire operated semaphore signal on the roof of the caboose, the locomotive driver is given the clear signal by the flagman to proceed forward or the warning of a red danger signal to stop.

Although the number of operational steam trains has reduced in recent years, there are still some excellent photographic opportunities to be had. There were few restrictions on where one could go to photograph the trains, the blue loader area inside the open pit, where the trains load up with coal, being one of them.

OPERATIONS
Open Pit

The western part of the opencast mine is operated by dump trucks which bring coal from the opencast workings to conveyor belts that feed the Xikeng loading pads. The loading pads are served by four lines, one to a large coal-loading facility (the blue loader), the second to a smaller, yellow-coloured loader and the others to pads fed by electric shovels. The number of trains working varied, but on a busy shift, a train could be seen every 20 minutes or so. Up to four trains could be seen in the pit at any one time; one arriving with empty hoppers, two loading up with coal and one departing loaded with coal. There could also be periods of inactivity lasting several hours depending on operational constraints, for example, mechanical failures at the loading pads.

The loaded trains, comprising 13 tipper wagons, each with a carrying capacity of 34 tons of coal, depart the pit, chimney first, going to the wash plant (washery) at Xuanmeichang, or, when in use, to the second coal

Diary extract – 5 December 2015

We arrive at Sandaoling late in the afternoon from Beijing, having flown up to Hami, about 60km away. There is no time to waste – we head straight off to the open pit coal mine. We are lucky, the pit is busy with four steam locomotives active. The sun is setting, giving rise to golden rails and backlit silhouetted trains. In the distance, I can hear the unmistakable sound of a steam train approaching, enhanced by the echo and reverberation off the pit walls. The JS Class locomotive works hard as it pulls its pay-dirt, 13 loaded wagons of coal, out of the deep man-made chasm accompanied by trailing steam and smoke. There is some wheel slippage as the locomotive climbs the gradient out of the pit towards the surface and momentarily loses traction, but due to the amazing skills of the driver, it soon recovers. Steam emits horizontally at boiler pressure from the engine for a short while as the driver opens the cylinder drain cocks, adding to the drama. It is more like a living, breathing creature than a man-made machine, a delight to see. This is a fantastic start to my first visit to Sandaoling and it is just the beginning!

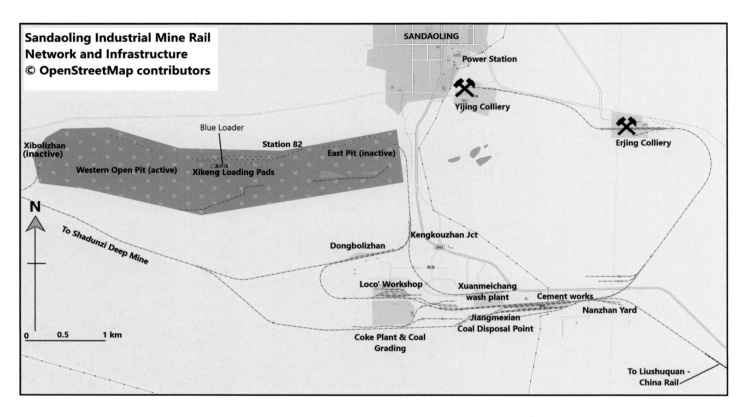

Sandaoling Industrial Mine Rail Network and Infrastructure © OpenStreetMap contributors

discharge point at Jiangmexian. When the coal has been discharged, the trains push back (reverse) to the pit to load up again. The train crews work 12-hour shifts and, assuming there are no operational constraints, can make six to seven trips to the pit each shift. I was particularly fortunate on my 2017 trip to be able to take a cab ride from Dongbolizhan down into the pit to the loading pads at Xikeng where the train loaded up with coal for the return trip to the washery – an experience I shall never forget.

There are some excellent photo opportunities when a train departs Xikeng fully laden with coal. The locomotives work hard as they slowly make their way from the loading pads, which can sometimes lead to wheel slippage and frequently results in dramatic exhaust-smoke plumes, making for some gritty industrial scenes. The eastern part of the open pit, now inactive, is also a good location to shoot steam action. At this stage, the trains gain a little speed, up to 30kph, as they ascend the pit to the surface for the wash plant at Xuanmeichang, a journey of approximately 7km.

Visibility at Sandaoling is often not that clear due to the vast amounts of dust produced by the mining operations, but if one is lucky enough to have a clear day, the Tian Shan Mountains, an extensive snow-capped mountain range, make for an impressive backdrop to the departing trains.

Another popular location for photographers within the pit is Ba'erzhan Station 82, about 1km east of Xikeng, which gives access to the loading area. It consists of a few huts and some strange-looking loudspeakers and is apparently named as a result of it being 82 metres below the surface of the open pit. Twilight shots, with the sun setting, are particularly atmospheric from this spot, but more elusive, and the real prize is capturing the showers of sparks that sometimes emanate from a locomotive, if one is lucky. Photographs in the golden glow as the winter sun sets over the open pit are also very desirable. Backlit exhausts, golden rails and silhouetted trains are a fine way to finish the day!

Dongbolizhan

This is where the locomotives take on water and undergo a checklist of tasks in preparation for the shift change. It is a popular spot for enthusiasts to take shots of the stationary locomotives during the shift change, in the morning (at around 0800) or during the evening. Recent years have seen a plethora of Chinese tourists gather at Dongbolizhan to photograph the morning spectacle.

Dawn is the optimum time to visit, especially about an hour or so before the sun rises if there is high pressure with clear skies as this gives a surreal experience under the stars in the cold, calm, serene conditions. A camera set up on a tripod at slow shutter speeds can deliver some stunning shots. Equally magical, is when the first of the sun's rays illuminate the locomotives giving rise to red skies and golden rails, not to mention a respite from the cold! Blowing down, when a vast cloud of steam is blown out with force from the side of the locomotive to clear out sludge from the bottom of the boiler, is also an impressive sight.

Coal Disposal Points

The trains finish their journeys from the open pit at one of two disposal points: Xuanmeichang and Jiangmexian.

The Xuanmeichang wash plant (washery) is the main location where the trains discharge their coal. The trains tip their hopper wagons into grates which feed a conveyor belt to the wash plant, where the coal is washed, crushed and graded. Two rail-mounted drag lines are sometimes used to clear the coal from the hoppers. Once processed, the coal is transferred from the yard at Nanzhan to the China state railway by diesel locomotive.

The washery is served by a single-line track that runs for approximately 2km from Kengkouzhan Junction, where the line descends into the open pit and branches to Dongbolizhan. After discharging the coal, the trains work hard on the climb up the short bank from the washery to Kengkouzhan Junction and then cruise down-grade as they descend into the pit to load up with coal again at Xikeng. Some wonderfully atmospheric shots, with impressive exhausts, accompanied by sparks if one is lucky, can be gained of the trains climbing the gradient to Kengkouzhan, especially in the low-light conditions at dusk or dawn.

Night or early morning shots of the trains discharging their payload at the washery are equally special, but daytime photography does not disappoint either. On occasion, spectacular exhausts are seen when the trains push away from the washery on their journey back to the pit.

On my second trip to Sandaoling in 2017, another disposal point was in use for the trains to discharge the coal from the open pit, at a place called Jiangmexian, approximately 0.4km south of the Xuanmeichang washery. It was thought the coal despatched to Jiangmexian was of an inferior quality compared to that brought to the washery at Xuanmeichang. It was stockpiled by conveyor belt for private sale without being processed and loaded into trucks for despatch. It is also feasible the coal could have been despatched by rail from Nanzhan using blue containers, which were seen at the yard.

A somewhat circuitous route is taken by the trains to get to the second disposal point. They exit the pit at Kengkouzhan Junction, pass through Dongbolizhan, then travel along a 180-degree curve past the workshop to reach another curve for the coke plant. From here, the trains push back (reverse) to Jiangmexian.

The use of the second disposal point at Jiangmexian was very welcome as it afforded some additional photographic opportunities. The dusty conditions and pollution, coupled with views of the Xuanmeichang washery and Nanzhan cement works, made for some powerful industrial scenes, providing a refreshing contrast to the open pit.

Underground Mines (Collieries)

There are two collieries, Yijing and Erjing, which are also referred to as No1 and No2 mines, respectively. Yijing is located near the town of Sandaoling and Erjing is about 3.5km east of the open pit. They are both served by a single-line track from Nanzhan Yard. At the time of my visits, there were no trains running to the Yijing Colliery, which is now reported to be no longer operational.

In contrast to the open pit operations, which use tipper wagons to haul the coal, the trains to Erjing use general purpose gondola wagons, which are loaded with coal for the return journey to Nanzhan. From Nanzhan, the loaded wagons are despatched to the national rail network at Liushuquan. Until October 2011, these trains were hauled by two JS Class locomotives, one at the front and a banker at the rear, with up to 60 wagons. Nowadays, they are now run by diesel locomotives.

The single-line track runs for approximately 5km from Nanzhan Yard to Erjing Colliery. The line heads in a north-easterly direction for about 2.7km and then curves west to the colliery. Despite no obvious signs of it, the line climbs a significant gradient to the point where it curves off to the colliery, so the trains hauling empty wagons from Nanzhan to the colliery have to work hard up the gradient, resulting in some notable exhausts. They operate on an intermittent basis, running tender first to the colliery and returning, chimney first, to Nanzhan. Longer trains are worked by pairs of JS Class locomotives, one at the front and a banker at the back. I was fortunate enough to see trains to and from Erjing on both my visits.

The line to Erjing traverses a bleak, featureless, arid landscape on the fringes of the Gobi Desert, so one might think that photographic opportunities are limited, but in fact the opposite is true. On a clear day, the snow-capped Tian Shan Mountains (also known as the Tengri Tagh or Tengir-Too, meaning 'Mountains of Heaven'), about 30km to the north, make for an impressive backdrop to an otherwise featureless terrain. Add to this a long train crossing the desert towards the mountains with up to 35 gondola wagons in tow, 'top and tailed' by two JS Class locomotives creating trailing exhausts as they negotiate the gradient, and you have the makings for some dramatic photography. Equally captivating, is the knowledge that these are the last banked steam trains to operate in the world, so are a sight to behold in the second decade of the 21st century.

Whilst the loaded coal trains lack exhaust as they make their way from the colliery down-grade back to Nanzhan, on a clear day, the view of the majestic Tian Shan Mountains more than makes up for this.

One of the last great hopes for additional steam outside the open pit was on the line to Shadunzi deep pit, west of Sandaoling. A new line commissioned in 2014 was expected to be worked by pairs of JS Class locomotives from Nanzhan. However, the dream never materialised. After a few test-runs with steam, the first trains to the colliery, hauling up to 50 gondola wagons, were powered by diesels. The massive trains have been running infrequently ever since, hauled by DF8 locomotives.

Workshop

Sandaoling has an impressive workshop, together with a foundry to fabricate parts, which I was able to visit. The facility has enabled steam to survive at the operation for many years and is likely the last steam workshop capable of heavy overhauls still operating in China. There are numerous old locomotives stored in a compound, essentially a graveyard, near the workshop. No doubt, many of the old locomotives have been striped and 'cannibalised' over the years to maintain the fleet of running locomotives. One great advantage, though, is that some of the locomotives can be made operational in a short time. This happened on my visit in 2017. One of the active locomotives, JS 8081, had to go to the workshop for a boiler washout (a procedure to wash out the boiler to remove scale and inspect the boiler and its components), but its loss of service did not impact on the operation. On the contrary, in

a noticeably short time, JS 8173, which looked like a rust bucket, was pulled out from the compound and was up and running in next to no time after some routine maintenance at the workshop. This is testament to the superb skill sets that exist at Sandaoling, which have resulted in a seamless operation over the years and perhaps is one of the reasons why steam traction has lasted for so long there. The skill sets are unique but will likely disappear altogether when the mine finally closes.

End of the line?

For years, railway enthusiasts have been debating when the steam railway will finally come to an end at Sandaoling. Factors such as how long the accessible coal reserves will last at the open pit, the practicality of using steam locomotives as opposed to replacing them with diesel locomotives or trucks to haul the final coal mined, steam boiler certification and the availability of staff with sufficient knowledge and experience to operate and maintain the industrial railway, have all come into play in the decision making.

However, as the mine is nearing the end of its productive life, there seems little point in investing in a new fleet of expensive diesel locomotives or using trucks to haul the coal. There is a workshop and foundry that can carry out heavy rebuilds on the locomotives and spare parts can easily be obtained from the graveyard of old locomotives, or retired locomotives can quickly be brought back into service. In addition, there is a workforce with the skills to keep the railway running. In a nutshell, if it works, why change it?

Each year, to the delight of rail enthusiasts, there has been a 'stay of execution'. Whilst it looks like 2020 may well see the end of the steam-hauled trains at Sandaoling, as I write, there are strong rumours circulating that they will continue until the end of 2021. So, perhaps there is one more opportunity to make another visit?

A view of the western (active) section of Sandaoling opencast coal mine with the mine benches visible in the background. In this scene, JS 8081 departs the pit loaded with coal for the wash plant. Meanwhile, another JS Class locomotive (behind) gets ready to depart the pit. Another train is being loaded with coal at the blue loader, as is evident from the smoke trail (centre right). 16 February 2017.

Opposite: A typical day at the western (active) part of the open pit at Sandaoling sees four JS Class locomotives in action. 5 December 2015.

JS 8167 heads a coal train destined for the wash plant, whilst JS 8081, to the left, waits to push back to the loading point to collect more coal. 8 December 2015.

JS 8190 works hard as it departs the open pit hauling another load of coal to the wash plant. 6 December 2015.

JS 8081, in the open pit at Sandaoling, hauls coal to the wash plant for processing. The Tian Shan mountains in the background are one of the longest mountain ranges in Central Asia, stretching some 2,900km east from Tashkent in Uzbekistan. 9 December 2015.

Opposite: The late afternoon sun illuminates the rich tones of the coal-bearing strata in the now defunct eastern part of the open pit at Sandaoling as JS 8081, seen on the left with a rake of empty wagons, pushes back to the loading bay at Xikeng. Meanwhile, JS 8197 makes haste in the opposite direction, laden with coal for the wash plant, whilst a lone photographer catches the action. 9 December 2015.

Double-headed JS Class loco-hauled trains are not a common sight at Sandaoling, but I was fortunate to witness one. With JS 8167 at the front and JS 8225 behind, which are seen leaving the pit, the unusual scenario was a result of some difficulties with JS 8225. 6 December 2015.

As the sun begins to set, smoke from smouldering coal can be seen in the background as the early evening light illuminates the open pit at Sandaoling and JS 8081 makes its way out of the mine with another load of coal destined for the wash plant. 8 December 2015.

JS Class locomotives load up with coal, for dispatch to the disposal points, at Xikeng in the western active part of the pit. The nearest train is headed by JS 8190. 18 February 2017.

Opposite: JS 8190 works hard as it departs the Xikeng loading bay with another load of coal for the wash plant. 18 February 2017.

JS activity is seen at Station 82, about 1km east of the loading pads in the active western part of the pit. Sandaoling operates on a push-pull basis. Empty tipper wagons are pushed back from the disposal points into the open pit to the loading pad at Xikeng, whilst loaded trains haul the coal, chimney first, back to the disposal points. 18 February 2017.

JS 8190 loads up with coal at the Xikeng loading pads as one of the train crew takes stock of the operation. 18 February 2017.

Opposite: JS 8167, in charge of 13 wagons laden with coal, catches the last of the sun's light as it exits the opencast coal mine at Sandaoling with another load of coal destined for the wash plant. Meanwhile, JS8081, in the background, waits for its path to push back to the loading point in the active western part (Xikeng) of the pit to load up with coal. 6 December 2015.

Right: As the sun begins to set, late-afternoon action sees JS 8167 departing the pit with coal for the washery at Xuanmeichang. Meanwhile, another train in the distance waits to push back to the loading pads, by the blue loader in the distance, to collect more coal. 5 December 2015.

Below: A JS Class locomotive takes on coal from the yellow loader in the western active part of the open pit at Xikeng. The orange-yellow glow to the left of the locomotive is a coal fire, a frequent occurrence at Sandaoling. 18 February 2017.

Another shot taken at Station 82, this time accompanied by night sparks. 18 February 2017.

Opposite: In the last of the light at Station 82, an unidentified JS Class locomotive departs the Xikeng loading pads with a loaded coal train for the wash plant. 8 December 2015.

A JS Class locomotive illuminates an otherwise pitch-black scene as it departs the open pit with another load of coal destined for the washery. A great deal of patience was required to get the shot. After many failed attempts, there was just about enough shutter speed to pull it off! 16 February 2017.

Opposite: The late afternoon sun illuminates the alien-looking landscape as a JS Class locomotive makes its way out of the open pit with another loaded coal train. 5 December 2015

A light engine is seen blowing down with night sparks at Dongbolizhan stabling yard. 16 February 2017.

A JS Class locomotive prepares for the morning shift at Dongbolizhan. 7 December 2016.

The morning line up at Dongbolizhan sees four JS Class locomotives prepare for the new shift. 17 February 2017.

A slow shutter speed gives a surreal feel to this scene at Dongbolizhan stabling yard as JS Class locomotives prepare for the new shift. 9 December 2015.

Shrouded in steam, JS 8167 gets ready for the new shift at Dongbolizhan as the early morning winter sun makes an appearance. 8 December 2015.

As the winter sun rises, JS Class locomotives push back empty tipper wagons from the stabling point at Dongbolizhan to collect coal from the open pit. 6 December 2015.

JS Class locomotive 8167 prepares for the new shift at Dongbolizhan before the sun rises. 9 December 2015.

Just before sunrise, JS 8197 prepares for the morning shift at Dongbolizhan.
9 December 2015.

Blowing down is when a vast cloud of steam is blown out with force from the side of the locomotive to clear out sludge from the bottom of the boiler. It is common practice at Dongbolizhan yard where the JS Class locomotives prepare for the morning shift. 14 February 2017.

Opposite: Taken at Dongbolizhan in early morning golden sunlight, the driver of 2-8-2 steam locomotive, JS8167, climbs to the footplate of the locomotive to commence the morning shift. 9 December 2015.

Every morning at Dongbolizhan, JS Class locomotives get ready for the morning shift. In this scene, one of the train crew roams about JS Class locomotive 8167 with his oil can, lubricating various places around the locomotive as part of the ritual dawn preparations. 8 December 2015.

Opposite: JS 8081, laden with coal, is directed onto the right line to discharge its coal at the Xuanmeichang washery. 8 December 2015.

Against the backdrop of the Tian Shan Mountains, JS 8197, with 13 tipper wagons loaded with coal, heads down-grade from Kengkouzhan Junction to the wash plant at Xuanmeichang.

Opposite: A lone figure photographs a JS Class locomotive pushing back a rake of empty coal hoppers from the washery to the open pit at Sandaoling. Some spectacular exhausts were observed as the trains pushed away up the short bank towards the pit. 14 February 2017.

I couldn't really have imagined sending this image as a postcard to somebody on my second visit to China saying, 'wish you were here!' That said, it gave me enormous pleasure to photograph the locomotives and heavy industry at Sandaoling. In this scene, JS 8081 discharges its train of coal from the open pit at the second disposal point (Jiangmexian) in Sandaoling. 14 February 2017.

Opposite: A 2-8-2 JS Class locomotive departs Jiangmexian, the second coal disposal point at Sandaoling, heading back to the open pit to collect more coal. A second JS Class locomotive can just be seen in the background (left) at the Xuanmeichang washery. 14 February 2017.

A JS Class locomotive pushes empty coal hoppers towards the open pit at Sandaoling to collect another load of coal for the washery. The abandoned mining town still survives for now, and some dwellings are still occupied. 15 February 2017.

Above: In the last of the light, an unidentified JS Class locomotive is seen pushing back a loaded coal train at the Xuanmeichang washery. 6 December 2015.

Right: A JS Class locomotive pushes back a rake of empty tipper wagons up the short bank to Kengkouzhan Junction where it will take the line to Dongbolizhan for the shift change. 16 February 2017.

Directed by the man with the green light, JS 8081 discharges coal from its tipper wagons at the Xuanmeichang washery early in the morning. 17 February 2017.

At Nanzhan, JS 8089 shunts gondola wagons used for the coal traffic to Erjing and Liushuquan. JS 6204 is seen in the background. 6 December 2015.

Right: Erjing Colliery is served by a single-track line that runs for approximately 5km from Nanzhan Yard. Despite no obvious signs of it, the line climbs a significant gradient to the point where it curves off to the colliery, so the trains returning empty wagons to the colliery work hard resulting in some notable exhausts. In this scene, JS8358 is seen departing Nanzhan as it makes its way across the featureless arid terrain with empty gondola wagons in tow to be filled up with coal at the colliery. 17 February 2017.

Below: JS 8314, with assistance from JS 8366 at the rear of the train, heads to Erjing Colliery across the flat, desolate, arid landscape with a long rake of gondola wagon. These are the last banked steam trains to operate in the world. 14 February 2017.

Above: In addition to the open pit operation at Sandaoling, steam trains also work coal trains to the nearby deep mine (colliery) at Erjing. In this scene, JS 8358 pulls a rake of empty gondola wagons across the spartan, arid landscape on the fringes of the Gobi Desert, banked by JS 8366 at the rear. The train is heading to the Erjing Colliery to collect coal for the return journey to Nanzhan Yard. 14 February 2017.

Left: The snow-capped Tian Shan Mountains punctuate an otherwise flat monotonous landscape on the fringes of the Gobi Desert. JS Class locomotive 8358, with 8366 bringing up the rear, works an empty coal train to the Erjing Colliery to collect coal for the return trip to Nanzhan Yard. From Nanzhan, the loaded wagons are despatched to the national rail network at Liushuquan by diesel. 17 February 2017.

Dwarfed by the snow-capped Tian Shan Mountains, JS Class steam locomotive 8366 runs light engine across the arid landscape towards the Erjing deep coal mine to collect a loaded coal train for the return journey to Nanzhan. 9 December 2015.

The snow-capped Tian Shan Mountains loom above JS Class locomotive 8366 and its loaded coal train as it makes its way back to Nanzhan Yard from Erjing Colliery. 9 December 2015.

Opposite: JS Class locomotives 8385 and 8366 (out of sight) prepare to take a loaded coal train to Nanzhan. 17 February 2017.

A JS Class locomotive pushes back a rake of empty coal hoppers to the open pit at Sandaoling past a secure compound and away from the main workshops and redundant JS and SY class locomotives that used to work the pit in busier times. Around 30 steam locomotives were operational during the 1990s. 14 February 2017.

A view inside the foundry. It's amazing to think of the skills and effort required to maintain the steam locomotives at Sandaoling, which will soon become history and be lost forever. 7 December 2015.

JS 8314 undergoes at boiler washout at the Sandaoling workshop. 7 December 2015.

Left: An elderly lady collects fallen coal from a level crossing. 18 February 2017.

Below left: The driver and his assistant check the firebox. 19 February 2017.

Below right: The driver of JS8225 catches a quiet moment whilst he fills in the log book during morning shift preparations at Dongbolizhan. 7 December 2015.

Opposite above left: The drivers and train crew were very friendly towards us. I was lucky enough to be invited to the footplate by this driver of JS 8190. 6 December 2015.

Opposite above right: The fireman takes a rest from shovelling coal while the driver controls the JS Class locomotive. 19 February 2017.

Opposite below left: Brewing up on a cold morning at Dongbolizhan. 14 February 2017.

Opposite below right: A JS Class locomotive passes through the old mining town of Sandaoling with coal destined for the washery. The old mining town still survives for now, abandoned, though some dwellings are still occupied as evidenced by these women who were walking up and down the street as part of their daily exercise routine. 15 February 2017.

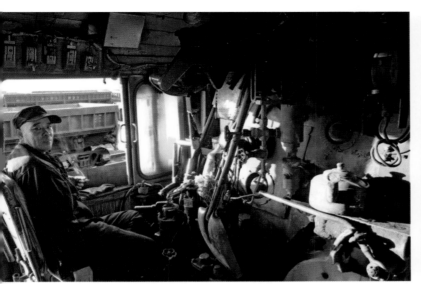

CHAPTER 2
FUXIN

Background

Fuxin is located in north-western Liaoning Province in north-east China, near the border with the Inner Mongolia Autonomous Region to the north. The region is richly endowed with coal resources which were first exploited during Qing times under the reign of the Daoguang emperor (1820–50) and then again during the Japanese occupation of Manchuria (1931–45).

During the 1950s, the mines were re-equipped and modernised. The Haizhou opencast coal mine, allegedly Asia's largest open pit, began operations in January 1951, employed up to 30,000 workers at its peak and had an annual production of three million tons. An extensive electric system once served the opencast mine and it supplied half of Fuxin's coal requirements for decades until its closure in 2005. A large thermal power station, once one of Asia's largest, was also built with Soviet aid in the mid-1950s and provides electricity to the regional power grid.

The Fuxin Mining Industry Group is a state-owned enterprise and the major coal mine owner in Fuxin. However, since 2001, several of the Fuxin Mining Industry Group's mines have been exhausted, leading to Fuxin's economic decline. This included the Haizhou open pit, which became bankrupt in 2005. The huge pit, 4km long, 2km wide and 700m deep, is the product of more than half a century of intensive mining, which produced some 244 million tons of coal.

Decades of coal mining has had a significant impact on the environment. Land subsidence, in particular, has been a major issue. Thousands of residents had to be evacuated from the estates built near the Haizhou open pit as engineers worked tirelessly to prevent them from collapsing and a major disaster was averted. Not surprisingly, Fuxin has been described as the 'sinking city' because of the unstable buildings under threat of collapse. It has also had to deal with decades of pollution from the coal mining and is currently trying to rectify its long-standing pollution problems. For decades, the huge Soviet-built power plant emitted sulphur dioxide (SO_2) directly into the city, resulting in residents suffering from chronic health problems. Newly installed SO_2 scrubbers at the plant have gone some way to resolving the issue.

There has been human tragedy too. There were at least 214 fatalities from an underground explosion at the Sunjiawan Colliery, which occurred shortly after an earthquake shook the mine in 2005. It was one of China's worst mine disasters in recent years. A rock burst accident at the Wulong Colliery caused another eight deaths in 2013, testament to the appalling and tragic mine safety record at Fuxin. Both mines were still in production at the time of my visit.

Most of Fuxin's mines have been gradually depleted since the 1980s, but coal continues to dominate the city's future. It is reported that the outlying mines produce around 20 million tonnes of coal a year, and the state power giant Datang Group is building a massive coal gasification plant in the city.

Diary extract – 29 November 2015

We travelled by train from Beijing to Jinzhou Nan and then by bus to Fuxin, about a five-hour journey, arriving at our hotel at around 9pm. After a tasty evening meal, not wanting to go straight to bed, I decided to try my luck with some night photography nearby. It was a surreal feel in the calm freezing conditions. The inimitable noise of not just one, but several, steam locomotives exuding vast plumes of steam as they worked hard, coupled with that unmistakable smell of burning coal, made me feel as if I had been propelled back in time.

I quickly set up my camera on a tripod in the hope of getting some respectable images of the moving trains. I cranked up the camera to ISO 6400, setting it to the widest aperture possible in the hope the shutter speed might just be sufficient to capture the moving trains in the dark – a tall order!

At around 11:30pm, I decided to call it a day and headed back to the warmth of the hotel. I took off my scarf, which felt as if it had been left it in the coldest part of a fridge for many hours (it was partly frozen), and looked at the RAW images on my camera screen with eager anticipation. I hoped that one or two might just be OK. I was not disappointed and was delighted with the results. Thank goodness I had brought a tripod with me!

OPERATIONS

Fuxin was the last operation in China where SY Class locomotives could be seen in number. At the time of my visit in 2015, 11 SY Class locomotives were in service, nine of them operational and two at the workshop as follows:

Locomotive Number	Comments
SY1195	
SY1210	
SY1319	
SY1320	
SY1378	In locomotive shop under repair.
SY1359	
SY1395	General Zhude logo.
SY1396	
SY1397	
SY1460	
SY1818	

There were two operating collieries with SY Class locomotives working at the mines: Wulong and Sunjiawan. Most of the coal production from the mines went directly to the power station but some of the coal was also despatched to the China State Railway sidings by diesel locomotive. The SY Class locomotives were also deployed to haul the mine waste from Wulong Colliery to a large tip behind the mine and to the defunct Haizhou open pit. Fly ash was also conveyed from Fuxin's power stations to the Wulong dump.

There was no shortage of steam action and consequently there were numerous photographic opportunities to be had in Fuxin. Most of the steam activity was of trains hauling mine waste and fly ash. Coal trains were not so common but were seen at some of the level crossings and at Wulong Colliery. At times, it seemed somewhat incongruous to see the trains passing the modern houses and apartments that have sprung up almost everywhere in Fuxin in recent years as a result of the modernisation of the city.

There were some cold, dull, dank, dreary mornings choked by smog with dismal visibility, exacerbated from burning coal at the power station, the exhaust from the steam engines and the windless still conditions. Pollution aside though, the dire, grimy conditions and poor visibility made for some wonderfully atmospheric shots.

Wulong Yard Stabling Point

For about an hour every morning after sunrise, up to six SY Class locomotives could be seen at the stabling point preparing for the new shift. The locomotive crews would light fires to keep themselves warm in between greasing wheels and carrying out general maintenance on the engines. In the still, cold, calm conditions, one was guaranteed to see spectacular plumes of steam billowing into the sky from the SY steam locomotives. On some days, it was almost as if they were in competition with Fuxin's main power station behind the yard, with its towering smoking stacks and cooling towers, which dominate the landscape.

Fuxin Depot

Located near the Fuxin Yard, the depot is where the locomotives took on water and sand, and cleaned out ash in preparation for the new shift. It was captivating to see these timeless procedures carried out by the crews almost half a century after steam was phased out in the UK.

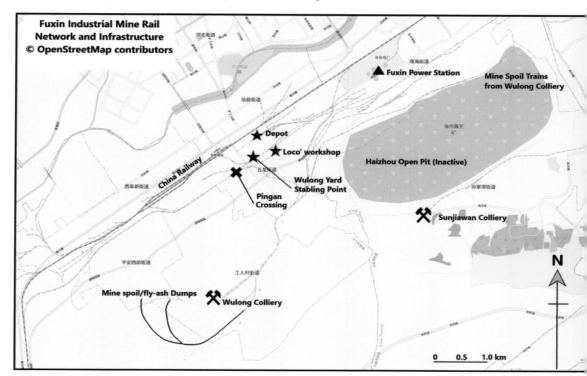

Night-time photography was particularly rewarding at the depot, especially of a locomotive over the ash pit in the low light. The trailing smoke and steam, the reflections in the puddles, the smell of burning coal and the train crews going about their final engine inspections before starting the new night shift are moments in time I shall never forget.

Fuxin Workshop

At the time of my visit, SY Class locomotives were still receiving major repairs and re-builds at the workshop located near the depot and stabling point. One locomotive was undergoing a major overhaul, whilst another, SY 1378, had just completed its repair and received a fresh coat of paint. Prior to starting the morning shift, several locomotives would make their way to the workshop for routine inspection checks and minor repair work.

DEEP MINES
Wulong Colliery

Served by two shafts, the colliery commenced production in 1957 and is reported to have produced two million tonnes of coal per annum. It remained operational until August 2016, when production stopped due to the mining company becoming bankrupt. Sadly, this resulted in the immediate cessation of the steam operation at Fuxin.

There were two train operations at the colliery – coal workings to the power station and mine waste trains hauling colliery spoil for dumping. The trains to the power station, which conveyed coal in gondola box wagons, were amongst the longest deployed at Fuxin. I believe some of the trains were also destined for the China State Railway, via Fuxin yard, worked by diesels.

On a cold, dull, dank morning, I was fortunate enough to see one coal train, hauled by SY 1320, depart the colliery for the power station. The dark conditions, together with the steam-laden atmosphere, made for a powerful industrial scene, perhaps reminiscent of one of the UK's former collieries, albeit with different steam traction and wagons.

In contrast to the coal trains, the mine waste trains were much shorter, hauling the waste in up to seven tipper wagons to the dumps. There were two locations where the colliery spoil was dumped: Wulong dump and Haizhou open pit.

Sunjiawan Colliery

This was also an important producing colliery at the time of my visit in 2015, located on the south-west side of the former Haizhou open pit mine. SY Class locomotives were deployed to haul the coal from the deep mine and I was able to photograph SY 1359 hauling a coal train on the edge of the old pit. As mentioned earlier, in 2005, the mine tragically suffered one of the worst mine disasters in China in recent years, with the loss 214 lives.

Wulong Dump

The dump, which forms a prominent hill in the surrounding countryside, is situated on the south-west side of the city and is the product of dumped underground mine rock waste and fly ash from power stations that has built up over decades. It is reached by a line that runs for approximately 4.5km from the colliery and branches at the top of the dump. To reach the dump, the spoil trains exit the colliery chimney first and then push back (reverse), tender first, up the steep gradient the line takes to reach the top level of the hill.

A couple of flagmen would accompany the trains in the open wagons at the rear. Their job was to warn the driver of danger as visibility is limited when the trains push back. It must have been a dreadful job as they were exposed to the freezing cold conditions in the winter months. However, far worse was being subjected to the vast plumes of dust from the tipped wagons without PPE (personal protective equipment), not even face masks, a potential recipe for serious chest diseases.

There were some superb photographic opportunities at the dump. The steep slow climb to the top resulted in some spectacular exhaust plumes as the locomotives worked hard to push the waste up the grade. Seeing the setting winter sun illuminating trailing steam/smoke plumes as the trains ascended the hill at a snail's pace, coupled with orangey pink skies, golden rails and the glint of the engines, was the highlight of my trip to Fuxin.

Haizhou Open Pit

Mine waste from Wulong Colliery was also dumped by trains into the former, non-operational, Haizhou open-pit mine. This huge scar in the earth's crust, which is up to 700m deep, was an ideal location to dispose of the waste. One could easily recognise these workings as they were usually slightly longer trains, comprising up to seven tipper wagons, operated on a push-pull basis. The loaded trains were pushed from the colliery by an SY Class locomotive, chimney first, to the old pit, with the empties pulled back to colliery tender first.

Fly Ash

In addition to the underground mine rock waste, fly ash from Fuxin's power stations was also dumped at Wulong dump. In previous years, prior to my visit, some of the fly-ash trains produced dust more akin to a volcanic eruption. I believe this massively polluting activity was stopped a few years ago by wetting the ash to reduce the pollution in the city. Whilst I did not witness such dramatic polluting scenes on my visit, voluminous quantities of dust were still produced during the ash tipping operations.

The trains comprised up to six tipper wagons, sometimes with a caboose at the rear of the train. Up to three men would ride in the caboose to operate the tippers. I believe some of the trains I photographed were from the Chengnan power station, located in the south-east part of the city. Some trains disposed of the ash at the lower levels of the dump, whilst others dumped the ash at the top level of the dump, overlooking the city. Again, there was no PPE for the workers, so the exposure to the toxic dust by the train crews must have been extremely hazardous for them.

Level Crossings

There are numerous level crossings in Fuxin, and they were always a good place to get pictures or simply observe the local folk. The best of these was Pingan crossing, which overlooked the Wulong Yard stabling point against the backdrop of the power station. Steam trains aside, it was a fascinating place to see the cross-section of the local life. Market traders displaying their street wares, people crossing the line on their way to work, smoking stacks, billowing smoke, cooling towers and steaming locomotives could all be construed as a Lowry composition.

For about an hour every morning after sunrise, up to six SY Class locomotives could be seen at the Wulong Yard stabling point preparing for the new shift. 1 December 2015.

Smog and pollution are all too common in China but the dire conditions made for some atmospheric shots. On a cold, dank, dull, dismal morning, SY Class locomotives prepare for the new day's shift at the Wulong stabling point near the workshop in Fuxin. 1 December 2015.

On a clear morning, five SY Class locomotives carry out their final locomotive checks before embarking on the new shift. SYs 1397, 1210 and 1359 are in the font of the line-up. 2 December 2015.

People cross the railway at Fuxin on their way to work, while SY steam locomotives 1395 and 1195 get up steam during preparations for the new morning shift. The locomotive on the left, SY1195, displays the portrait of General Zhu De, one of China's greatest military leaders and the founder of the Chinese communist army. 3 December 2015.

During the early morning shift change in the still, cold, calm conditions at Wulong Yard, one was guaranteed to see spectacular plumes of steam billowing into the sky from the SY steam locomotives. On some days, it was almost as if they were in competition with the towering smoking stacks and cooling towers from Fuxin's main power station, which dominate the scene behind. 2 December 2015.

An SY Class locomotive working a mine spoil train passes the steam locomotive workshop in morning smog. 1 December 2015.

SY 1210, pulls a coal train destined for the power station. Meanwhile, SY 1397, running light engine, departs the workshop to start the new shift. 1 December 2015.

Smoking stacks, billowing smoke, cooling towers, people crossing the line on their way to work. The stark conditions on a winter's day at Fuxin could be straight out of a Lowry painting but, alas, they are scenes from contemporary China. 3 December 2015.

Opposite: SY Class locomotives prepare for the morning shift at Fuxin Depot. 4 December 2015.

Three SY Class locomotives prepare for night duties at Wulong Yard. 2 December 2015.

Above: SY Class locomotive 1460 blows down at Wulong Yard, against the backdrop of the towering stacks from Fuxin's Soviet-built coal-fired power station. 2 December 2015.

Right: Two SY Class locomotives stand side by side at Wulong Yard getting ready to depart for the new shift. 1195 is on the left (with a picture at the front of a Chinese general) and 1395 is on the right. The SY Class was China's standard industrial locomotive. Over 1,800 of these useful light 2-8-2s were built between 1960 and 1999, the vast majority at Tangshan. 3 December 2015.

SY Class locomotives 1396 and 1320 are seen outside the workshop in Fuxin undergoing minor maintenance, whilst on the right, SY 1397 heads a spoil train. 2 December 2015.

Above left: SY Class Locomotive 1396 departs the workshop at Fuxin having undergone minor repairs. 1 December 2015.

Above right: A solitary worker and locomotive are seen at the entrance to the steam locomotive workshop. 1 December 2015.

Below left: The driver of SY 1460 greases the wheels of his locomotive in preparation for the new shift at Wulong Yard. 2 December 2015.

Below right: At the workshop in Fuxin, SY Class locomotive 1378 almost looks new after a rebuild and a new coat of paint. 1 December 2015.

SY Class locomotives, seen at the steam depot in Fuxin, prepare for the night shift. The word on the red neon sign translates into 'BaoDi Cheng' (or 'BaoDi City'), which means the residential area is a treasure place. 1 December 2015.

Opposite: SY Class locomotives preparing for the new night shift at the depot. 1 December 2015.

A view of Wulong Colliery. The mine, which had been in production since 1957, was reported to produce two million tonnes of coal per annum and remained in operation until August 2016, when the colliery was declared bankrupt. This resulted in the immediate cessation of the steam operation at Fuxin. 4 December 2015.

Opposite: Located near the Fuxin Yard, the depot is where the locomotives took on water and sand, and cleaned out ash in preparation for the new shift. It was captivating to see these timeless procedures carried out by the crews almost half a century after steam was phased out in the UK. In this scene, SY Class locomotive 1397 gets ready to leave the depot to start the new shift. 1 December 2015.

SY Class locomotive 1320 prepares to leave Wulong underground coal mine heading a coal train likely destined for the power station at Fuxin. The scene is perhaps reminiscent of one of the UK's former collieries during the steam era, albeit with different steam traction and wagons. 3 December 2015.

Opposite: SY 1359 works a loaded coal train from Sunjiawan Colliery, located on the south side of the huge defunct Haizhou opencast coal mine, allegedly Asia's largest opencast mine. Fuxin's Soviet-built power station dominates the background on the north side of the pit. 2 December 2015.

The cold, dull, dreary, dank conditions meant that two locomotives were required to move mine waste to Wulong dump due to adhesion problems. 1 December 2015.

Opposite: SY 1460 pushes back a train of mine spoil waste from the nearby Wulong Colliery. The tracks were very slippery at the level crossing, giving rise to wheel slippage as locomotives tackled the steep grade, often resulting in spectacular plumes of exhaust smoke and steam. 2 December 2015.

On a cold, dull, dismal day, SY Class locomotive 1460 discharges its load of power station fly ash at Wulong dump. This was a dreadful job for the men tipping the ash without PPE. 1 December 2015.

Mine underground waste and fly ash tipping operations were entirely carried out by SY Class steam locomotives at Fuxin. Making its way up the steep incline, an unidentified SY Class locomotive pushes another load of mine waste to be dumped. Wulong Colliery and Fuxin's main power station are the backdrop to the scene. 3 December 2015.

An SY Class locomotive pushes back tipper wagons loaded with fly ash from Chengnan power station to be dumped at the tip. Wulong underground mine and Fuxin's main power station can be seen behind the train. The man in front of the caboose, and two others, will help tip the load, an incredibly hazardous job. 2 December 2015.

Above: The Wulong dump, a man-made hill, composed of fly ash from power stations and underground mine waste, commands a fine view of Fuxin city. In this scene, SY Class locomotive 1359 discharges another load of fly ash. The operations ceased in 2016 as a result of the closure of Wulong Colliery. 3 December 2015.

Left: Wulong dump, high above Fuxin city, is composed of decades-worth of fly ash and mine waste. In this scene, SY Class locomotive 1359 discharges its load of fly ash. 3 December 2015.

Opposite: SY 1320 discharges mine rock waste from Wulong Colliery at the Wulong dump. It was a hazardous occupation for the train crew working without PPE. 2 December 2015.

Taken in late-afternoon winter light as the sun begins to set, an unidentified SY Class locomotive completes the steep climb to the top of Wulong dump to dispose of its train of underground mine waste. 2 December 2015.

Opposite: SY 1460 catches the glint of the setting winter sun as it pushes back up the incline to dispose of mine spoil in the barren wasteland. 3 December 2015.

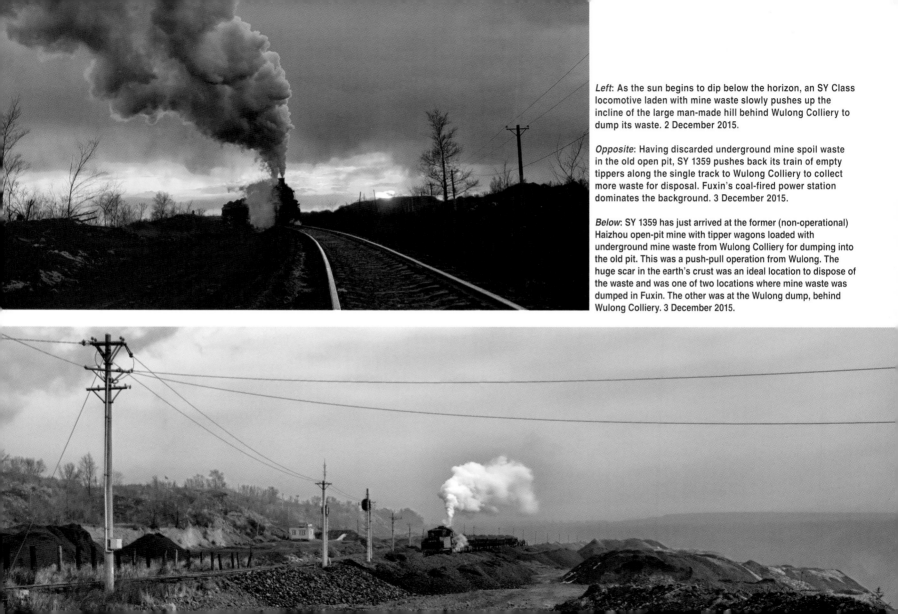

Left: As the sun begins to dip below the horizon, an SY Class locomotive laden with mine waste slowly pushes up the incline of the large man-made hill behind Wulong Colliery to dump its waste. 2 December 2015.

Opposite: Having discarded underground mine spoil waste in the old open pit, SY 1359 pushes back its train of empty tippers along the single track to Wulong Colliery to collect more waste for disposal. Fuxin's coal-fired power station dominates the background. 3 December 2015.

Below: SY 1359 has just arrived at the former (non-operational) Haizhou open-pit mine with tipper wagons loaded with underground mine waste from Wulong Colliery for dumping into the old pit. This was a push-pull operation from Wulong. The huge scar in the earth's crust was an ideal location to dispose of the waste and was one of two locations where mine waste was dumped in Fuxin. The other was at the Wulong dump, behind Wulong Colliery. 3 December 2015.

SY 1359 passes the manned crossing pulling empty tipper wagons destined for Wulong underground mine, which will be filled up with more waste for the return trip. The smoking stacks of Fuxin's coal-fired power station are seen in the background. 3 December 2015.

In freezing cold night conditions, an unidentified SY Class locomotive is seen working one of the many mine waste trains in Fuxin. 29 November 2015.

SY 1359 begins night-shift duties. 2 December 2015.

Opposite: An SY Class locomotive is illuminated by an approaching diesel locomotive. 29 November 2015.

SY 1395, displaying the portrait of General Zhu De, one of China's greatest military leaders and the founder of the Chinese communist army, gets the yellow flag to proceed past the crossing. It is working a fly-ash train from Chengnan power station, located in the south-east part of the city. 3 December 2015.

Opposite: SY 1359 crosses one of the many level crossings in Fuxin, hauling coal, possibly from Sunjiawan Colliery, destined for the China State Railway, via Fuxin yard. 3 December 2015.

Overshadowed by the smoking stacks from the power station in the background, folk cross the line on their way to work. This was a typical early-morning winter scene at Fuxin in 2015. 4 December 2015.

Whilst the gate keeper keeps a lookout, an SY Class locomotive, in charge of empty mine spoil tipper wagons, pushes back through the level crossing en route to Wulong Colliery. 3 December 2015.

Above: Market traders display their street wares early in the morning as people head for work whilst two SY Class locomotives pass by. 3 December 2015.

Right: The driver of SY 1460 does not appear best pleased at being photographed. 2 December 2015.

CHAPTER 3
BAIYIN

Background

Baiyin is an industrial city located north of the city of Lanzhou in Gansu Province on the upper reaches of the Yellow River, which flows from south to north through Baiyin Prefecture, though does not flow through the city. It is bordered by Ningxia Hui autonomous region to the east and Inner Mongolia to the north.

Geographically, Baiyin is in an arid, semi-desert area with extremely low rainfall. It is situated at the transition of the Qilian Mountains and Loess Plateau. The distinctive Loess Plateau is composed of very fine-grained, wind-deposited alluvium, highly friable material deposited by windstorms known as loess, which is the German word for loose. The deposits attain thicknesses of up to 80m (260ft) and mask the underlying surface. In Chinese, it is known as *huángtǔ*, 'yellow earth'.

The name, Baiyin (白銀), translated into English, means silver. The area has a long history of mining, which began as early as the Han Dynasty (206BC–AD220). Referred to as the 'treasure land', the mining industry had reached its pinnacle there by the Ming Dynasty (1368–1644). During this time, Baiyin became a city famed for its Baiyin Factory, an official institution that controlled the excavation of gold and silver and the subsequent distribution of the precious metals under a Government-run monopoly. Taking the official name 'Good Silver', Baiyin is the only city named after a noble metal in Chinese history.

In the 1950s, geologists from the Chinese geological bureau began systematic exploration in an area surrounding historic mines and discovered that the area was rich in copper, lead and zinc with precious metal credits, including gold and silver. The work lead to the discovery of the Baiyinchang ore field where four volcanogenic massive sulphide deposits were discovered. Since 1956, the ore field has produced copper, lead, zinc and precious metals from the four deposits. The Zheyaoshan copper deposit in the north was the largest but is now mined out. The third largest, Xiaotieshan, is a rich copper-lead-zinc deposit exploited in an underground mine, which feeds the ore to the Sanyelan smelter via an overhead cable line.

Operations

The Baiyin Nonferrous Metal Corporation (now known as the Baiyin Nonferrous Group Co. Ltd) operates the mines and smelters in the ore field and at Baiyin and produces copper, aluminium, lead, zinc, gold and silver products. The company is one of China's leading zinc producers and used to be the main copper supplier in China.

The operation is served by a private railway, run by the Baiyin Nonferrous Metal Corporation, which links the mines, plants and smelters. It runs 10km out of the industrial area at Baiyin Gongsi and into the mountains, running north to reach the Sanyelan smelter (that produces lead-zinc concentrates) and the Kuangsan copper mine further north. The steeply graded line that traverses the Loess Plateau is the only known line into the Loess mountains.

Until 2009, the industrial railway was worked using a small fleet of SY steam locomotives working ore, chemical and passenger trains. Steam trains hauled ore, or yellow sulphuric acid tanks, in the grimy,

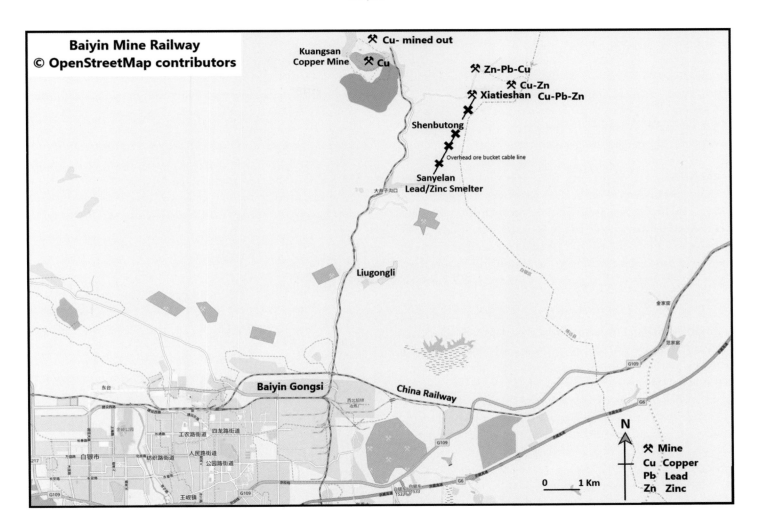

Baiyin Mine Railway
© OpenStreetMap contributors

⚒ Cu- mined out

Kuangsan
Copper Mine   ⚒ Cu

⚒ Zn-Pb-Cu
⚒ Cu-Zn
⚒ Xiatieshan   Cu-Pb-Zn

Shenbutong

Overhead ore bucket cable line

Sanyelan
Lead/Zinc Smelter

Liugongli

Baiyin Gongsi   China Railway

N

⚒ Mine
Cu Copper
Pb Lead
Zn Zinc

0   1 Km

stark, polluted industrial sprawl at Baiyin Gongsi, a favourite spot for rail enthusiasts to visit in China. The smelters, slag heaps and plant complexes, coupled with the tall stacks belching out smoke into grey polluted skies, made for some hard-core gritty industrial scenes.

However, perhaps the biggest prize of all was to capture one of the steam-hauled passenger, or ore, trains along the scenic line to the mines in the north. Every day, five passenger trains used to run each way between Baiyin and Shenbutong, ferrying workers from Baiyin Gongsi's railway station to the makeshift stations in the mining area. These were amongst the last of the regular passenger commuting services powered by steam locomotives in the world but this was all to change. The first diesels arrived at Baiyin in 2010, which inexorably signalled the end of the steam trains. The lack of spare parts to keep the locomotives running did not help the situation and inevitably meant that other SYs had to be striped and 'cannibalised' to maintain the few in operation.

The passenger services were finally discontinued on 20 November 2015, when four diesel locomotives were purchased that month by the Baiyin Nonferrous Metal Corporation, so ending the era of steam at Baiyin. However, this was not quite the end of the story. The mine workers complained of being cold on the new diesel-hauled trains, so a steam locomotive continued to operate at the rear of the train in the winter months to heat up the carriages. The practice continued through the winter months in 2016 and into early 2017.

On our visit to Baiyin, we missed the last official steam-hauled passenger train to Kuangsan by just three weeks, but all was not lost. On the morning of 11 December 2015, the mine workers passenger train arrived back at Baiyin Gongsi, having dropped off the mine workers at Shenbutong. It was headed by DF7G diesel locomotive, 5183, with SY 1583 trailing at the rear of the train to provide heat for the carriages. This was the last working steam locomotive in Baiyin, and it survived until early 2017.

To my delight, Bernd Seiler, of FarRail Tours, managed to organise the return of the train to Shenbutong, just a couple of hours later, with SY 1583 providing the motive power, which gave us the opportunity to photograph it winding through the mountains.

Diary extract – 11 December 2015
We clambered up the steep hills to reach the vantage point looking down onto the line that weaves its way through the Loess Plateau. The unique scenery the line traverses is awe inspiring with its rounded yellow hills in the spartan arid landscape. The weather was clear and the sun was behind our shoulders, so we had ideal conditions for the shots. We waited with eager anticipation to see the train as it climbed the gradient through the hilly country. It finally emerged, hauling six grubby passenger carriages, with an impressive head of steam. The striking landscape made for a superb backdrop as the steam train snaked and climbed its way through the hilly terrain.

Opposite: SY 1583 was, I believe, the last active SY Class locomotive at Baiyin. 10 December 2015.

The last official steam-hauled passenger train carrying workers from Baiyin to Kuangsan copper mine ran on 20 November 2015. After that, the trains were diesel-hauled. However, the workers complained of cold carriages so the sole surviving operational steam locomotive at Baiyin, SY 1583, was attached to the rear of the train to provide heat to the carriages. In this scene, the train has just returned to Baiyin, having transported the workers to the mines with diesel locomotive DF7G at the front and steam locomotive SY 1583 at the rear. This practice continued until early 2017, when the steam was discontinued. 11 December 2015.

Almost looking like a toy train, SY 1583 is seen shunting wagons of sulphuric acid at Baiyin Gongsi in this heavily industrialised location. 10 December 2015.

Left: SY Class steam locomotive 1583 gets up steam as it departs Baiyin for the Kuangsan copper mine. 11 December 2015.

Opposite: SY 1583 heads a passenger train though the rounded yellow hills of the Loess Plateau on the industrial line from Baiyin, which serves the copper-lead-zinc mines to the north and the Senyalen smelter. The operation is now run by diesel locomotives. 11 December 2015.

Below: Deployed to carry workers of the China Nonferrous Metal Mining Company to Kuangsan copper mine, SY Class steam locomotive 1583 is seen departing Baiyin in the grimy industrial surroundings. 11 December 2015.

SY 1583, in charge of empty coaching stock, winds its way through the arid hilly terrain of the Loess Plateau to the mine complex run by the Baiyin Nonferrous Metal Corporation. The yellow rocks in the distance, to the right, relate to mining operations from the Kuangsan copper mine. 11 December 2015.

Opposite: SY 1583, deployed to carry workers for the China Nonferrous Metal Mining Company, climbs through the mountains between Shenbutong and Kuangsan, passing an old tunnel, a relic of the former line. 11 December 2015.

SY 1583, deployed to carry workers for the China Nonferrous Metal Mining Company, is seen in the arid hilly terrain heading between Shenbutong and Kuangsan. 11 December 2015.

CHAPTER 4
WU JIU

Wu Jiu is in Inner Mongolia, 120km north-east of the large city of Hailar and 58km north-east of the county-level city of Yakeshi, whose economy is based on agriculture, forestry and mining. Its existence as an industrial steam railway serving collieries has only been known about in recent years.

The long trek to this isolated part of Inner Mongolia was a punt as there was no guarantee that steam trains would be working. An additional complication was the fact that the operation was further hampered by the absence of wagons, as the mining operation does not own any of its own wagons and, consequently, they need to be loaned out from China Rail. It was therefore a huge gamble to travel this far without the assurance of witnessing a steam locomotive in action. However, the lure of visiting another new location in China, with snow in harsh winter sub-zero temperatures, was compelling. We were in luck as there were wagons, and one steam locomotive was in operation.

Temperatures during the visit dropped down to around -30 degrees Celsius at night and, I suspect, were not that much different during the day. Not surprisingly, Wu Jiu has aptly been described as Siberia in all but name. The allure of seeing a steam train in the low winter sunlit still conditions, in snow under clear skies, with the likelihood of some stunning steam effects, could not be resisted.

Operations
The Wu Jiu Coal Group Company Ltd, who operate the mines and railway, had three SY Class locomotives and one diesel locomotive at the locomotive shed, all in particularly good condition. SY 1225 was building up steam in the shed ready for the day's work ahead.

Locomotive Number	Comments
SY1546	
SY1134	
SY1225	Operational.
DF4DD 0288	Operational.

There are four collieries (deep mines) at Wu Jiu, connected by the mine railway, which heads west to Metianzhen, where the line connects to China Rail's Yakeshi to Yitulihe line. Number 4 Colliery to the south is a relatively new deep mine where most of the steam activity currently takes place. The steam operation can be described as sporadic at best, operating on an as and when required basis, sometimes at night. As mentioned, the main encumbrance to the whole operation is the lack of gondola wagons to haul the coal as this is contingent on the availability of China Rail wagons in the Yakeshi/Haila'er area. Until a few years ago, an SY Class locomotive was deployed to haul the wagons from Metianzhen to the collieries. Nowadays, however, the DF4DD diesel locomotive is used for this task.

The last reported steam activity at Wu Jiu was in November 2017. Since then, as far as I am aware, there have not been any recorded sightings of steam, so the current status of the operation is unknown.

Diary extract – 21 February 2017

The train is coming towards us from the No3 Colliery with a rake of gondola wagons. The line follows the road in the open, gently undulating terrain blanketed in snow, passing the wooden chalets and brick-built dwellings with their smoking chimneys and snow-clad roofs. As hoped for, the bitterly cold conditions result in mightily impressive vertical plumes of steam as the train slowly makes its way along the line. To avoid changing lenses and losing valuable time, I have two cameras around my neck to capture the action, one with a 55-200mm telephoto zoom lens and the other with an 18-55mm lens, but I keep getting an error message on my digital camera. I frantically try to determine how the solve the problem – the solution is to take the battery out of the camera, warm it in my hands for 20 seconds or so and pop it back in the camera – it works! I have the camera set to burst so that I can get as many shots as possible before it freezes over again. I am not sure how cold it is but would hazard a guess it is around -20 degrees. The train was only active for a few hours, but we were fortunate enough to be able to photograph it at several locations.

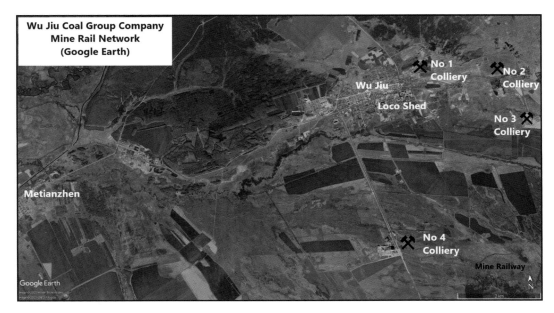

It was long way to travel to witness steam in action over such a short time. Nevertheless, it was absolutely thrilling to see a steam train in another part of China in the harsh winter conditions, perhaps reminiscent of a bygone age when such winter scenes were all too common on the China Rail network.

Diesel locomotive D4DD-0288 stands next to SY Class locomotive 1225, both owned by the Wu Jiu Coal Group. 21 February 2017.

In the freezing cold conditions, SY 1225 pushes a rake of empty box wagons towards No3 Colliery on the Wu Jiu Coal Group line, which parallels the road. 21 February 2017.

Opposite: Another winter scene on the Wu Jiu Group coal line. 21 February 2017.

This image, taken in bitterly cold conditions, shows SY 1225 with a rake of empty box wagons on the Wu Jiu Coal Group line. 21 February 2017.

Opposite: In bitterly cold conditions, SY 1225 is seen with a rake of gondola wagons on the Wu Jiu Coal Group line. 21 February 2017.

SY 1125 passes wooden chalets and brick-built dwellings, with their smoking chimneys and snow-clad roofs, as it makes its way from the No3 Colliery to Wu Jiu. 21 February 2017.

Opposite: In freezing conditions, SY 1225 pushes up an incline with an impressive head of steam as it follows the road-hauling box wagons. 21 February 2017.

SY 1225 collects coal at the No1 Colliery.
21 February 2017.